PEACE FOR UKRAINE, NOW!

POEMS AND COMMENTS BY
DR. RICHARD COOK

First Edition: *Peace for Ukraine, Now!* by Dr Richard Cook.

ISBN: 978 1 7396674 1 2

Cover drawings by and copyright Philip Hewitson.

First published in the UK in 2023 by Caldew Press.

Caldew Press
Tolivar
12 St George's Crescent
Carlisle
CA3 9NL

www.caldewpress.com

Printed by 4edge Ltd, UK.

CALDEW PRESS

PEACE FOR UKRAINE, NOW!

Poems and Comments by

Dr. Richard Cook.

INTRODUCTION

Welcome to one and all who consider the dreadful war in the Ukraine to be a travesty perpetrated by an evil despot. The situation is desperate and anything we can do to shorten the time in conflict and bring the tyrant to justice will be appreciated. This is my small effort to at least make the situation something that is in the collective consciousness now and for as long as it takes. I have nothing but admiration for their leader Volodymyr Zelenskyy and the way he has conducted himself in the direst of circumstances; he was a comedian before he entered the political arena, our politicians should take note and use his example of honesty, decency and integrity in the face of danger.

Since the invasion I have been moved by the plight of the innocent men, women and children of this proud nation to put some of my feelings down on paper and as a result this volume of recent and original poems has come to fruition.

The first fifteen are directly related to Russia and the Ukraine, the rest are ones I have been writing over the last twelve months and I hope you will enjoy the sentiments. There are some with earlier dates but they are ones I started a while ago and have only recently completed.

I feel that I have an affinity with the Ukrainians, my father was born in a town called Jarosław, in the south-eastern part of Poland and very close to the border with Ukraine. When the Second World War broke out in 1939, my father was studying law at the university in Vilnius, the Russians moved in from the east while the Germans were attacking the west. He spent the next three years in a Siberian labour camp. Unsurprisingly he did not like the Russians then under Stalin and I doubt he would have much time for the present leader.

This book is dedicated to the people of Ukraine who have died unnecessarily as the result of the conflict perpetrated by Russia and Putin.*

*I have no wish to honour this person with even a title.

TABLE OF CONTENTS.

INDEX OF FIRST LINES.

35. I squat right down.
36. You begin as an amorphous blob.
37. We trip the light fantastic.
38. It's like a sport, when fuel is short.
39. Be a positive force, in a negative world.
40. A gaggle of geese, waddle along the road.
41. That first moment, a breath, a gasp, a cry…
42. The sharpest of all weapons is the tongue.
43. Enormous tusks and giant bones.
44. Inflation, it's good for balloons.
45. They'd like to see them endangered, like the panda.
46. Talk about tomorrow?
47. Are we alone in the universe?
48. Can it be a particle?
49. There was a man called Ranter.
50. Well they loved so much.
51. There's no turkey this year, bird flu took care of that.
52. So, I'm looking for a warm space.
53. Straining every sinew
54. When all your troubles make you numb.

1. PEACE FOR UKRAINE, NOW! (2022)

Just thinking about this topic and the title of the book of poems I was obliged to write a poem with the title "Peace in Ukraine, now!" The war has been ongoing for twelve months and the number of atrocities and war crimes that Putin (I refuse to use his title or first name) and his Russia have committed is beyond belief. He will not win, he must be aware of that, yet arrogant pride stops him beating a retreat or making a truce.

Stop the war, we don't wish to be Russia!
We're Ukrainian and proud of our land.
We remember when our fields were lusher,
Civilians weren't bombed, we don't understand.

    Bring peace to Ukraine
    Though we don't know how,
    We love our nation,
    Peace for Ukraine, now!

Cease bombing the buildings, once homes of course;
Leave the Crimea and lands that aren't yours.
From the East and North the invading force,
You should not be here, for you have no cause.

    Send love to Ukraine
    Make a solemn vow,
    Defend our nation
    Peace for Ukraine, now!

Ban missiles, aimed at us to try and kill
Our people and our spirit around Kyiv.
We don't want to fight, but certainly will,
Till every last Russian is forced to leave!

2. RETURN OF THE RED ARMY. (2022)

The Workers' and Peasants' Red Army, usually shortened to the Red Army, was established in 1918 and is the army and air force of the Russian Soviet Federative Socialist Republic and after 1922 the USSR. It was disbanded following the Second World War in 1946. It was said that you could smell them before you could see them (I am not sure if it was the horses or the fact their hygiene was low on their list of duties). Now Putin is mobilising troops, mainly young boys who have no idea what they are letting themselves in for.

There's a massive presence massing
On the borders of Ukraine,
Putin says it's an exercise –
We know it's against the grain.
There's troops and planes and battleships
Cruising close to Crimea.
It may seem normal in Kiev,
But the people live in fear!
      It's the return of the Red Army
      They'll always get you out of a spot;
      But starting World War Three is barmy,
      So, let's see who will fire that first shot!

While back in the 1930s
Under a brutal regime,
A collective farming policy
Released industrial steam.
Though it proved unsustainable
How peasants tried to please.
But corruption, poor management,
Then drought, brought them to their knees.
      It's the return of the Red Army,
      They only obey orders I'm told.
      But killing innocents is barmy
      The war now heats up, no longer cold.

Four million died of starvation,
Just a tragic consequence?

For one death is a tragedy,
But that number makes no sense.
It's put down as a statistic –
Every life lost is one too much;
It's when dictators bend the rules,
That's when they lose the human touch!
    It's the return of the Red Army,
      Can't blame soldiers, it's the men at the top.
      More deaths on their conscience is barmy,
      I wonder when it will all stop?

We must negotiate for peace,
Hope and pray, will no one back me?
Yet still more troops are arriving
And submarines in the Black Sea.
They're getting worried in Donetsk,
There's little love in Lviv;
We must strive for peace at all costs
For there's nothing else to give!
    It's the return of the Red Army,
      A ruthless hoard coming from the east.
      No thought of peace or love, that's barmy,
      But that is the nature of the beast!

Is it ever too late for peace,
And call off the dogs of war?
The refugees are fleeing fast –
Will the West open the door?
Bullets fly, and bombs are falling,
Tanks roll in, jets fly overhead.
How the innocent will suffer,
Does it end when they're all dead?
    The Red Army's on the march again,
      This time for real and there will be blood!
      They've invaded a state, for terrain,
      This is war, and it is never good.

3. CRASS-PUTIN! (2022)

This is a pun on Grigori Rasputin 1869-1916, the evil so called 'mad monk' who was at the court of the Russian Tsar Nicholas II. He was a mystic, visionary and prophet, although he had no official position in the Russian Orthodox church. Others thought he was a charlatan and plotted to do away with him. Eventually he was poisoned with cakes laced with cyanide, shot three times at close range and finally tossed off a bridge into the river Malaya Nevka and drowned. Obviously a difficult man to dispose of which is something he has in common with the current leader of Russia!

Putin, put out?
No! But so many are in Ukraine,
You wield such power with so little brain;
Even your own people see no gain.

Putin, put off?
Sadly not! Do his vile thoughts not end?
Is he possessed, or just round the bend?
We're all in danger from this bad trend.

Putin, put down
Your weapons, strive for peace in the world,
There's no point with all those missiles hurled;
Everywhere blue and yellow unfurled.

Putin, put away
Thoughts of hate, for they will never win-
We stand together in love as kin.
You're deluded, whatever the spin!

Putin, put up
Your hands and give up – your plans are wrong!
You are so weak, though you think you're strong,
These war crimes avenged before too long.

Putin, put back
Your armies, your planes and rolling tanks,
We will break you, your power and your banks.
Then the whole world will breathe grateful thanks.

4. WHAT'S NEW IN RUSSIA? (2022)

Well, there's nothing new, the leaders have always been paranoid despots with deranged plans. I rest my case.

We have a new policy in force,
"Kill first and don't think about it later!"
We never use the word war, of course,
It's for the brainwashed minds we cater.

We don't like to fight so we threaten,
We blame our enemies for the first strike,
The West for aiding and abetting
And we twist the truth, so what's not to like?

Now we've stopped the radio broadcast
And shut down the independent TV.
You can believe all you hear, at last
And really trust everything that you see.

We wonder where all the money went;
So, what's new in Russia, prices are high,
Strangely there's a lot of discontent,
Inflation is rampant, we puzzle why.

Our oligarchs are cash-strapped it seems,
Now we're fighting a war we can't afford.
Could this be the end of all our dreams?
Let's invade somewhere else, I'm getting bored!

The news in Russia may seemed biased,
The truth is written on scraps of paper!
Sometimes morals are not the highest,
So they all pretend it's just a caper.

Now if you happen to disagree
We have a place ready for dissenters.
For this is the country of the free!
Let's go and bomb some more city centres!!

5. OUR UKRAINE. (2022)

Occasionally I write poetry without rhymes, this is one that paints a picture from the Ukrainian perspective. The front cover of this book is supposed to represent the Ukrainian flag of blue and gold. Out of the blue sky the dove of peace flutters over the fields of ripening corn.

Our Ukraine should be in your thoughts;
Our flag is blue and gold, you now see it everywhere.
The blue represents the cloudless skies,
Now blackened with the smoke rising from exploded incendiary devices.
The gold for the wheat ripening in fields,
But who will be left here, to bring in the harvest?

Our Ukraine is being devastated.
Our cities are being demolished by missiles and air strikes.
Soldiers arrive in tanks and try to take our country from us;
We are a proud people and we will not go easily.
We have had a troubled past, a present that is worse and without help what future do we have?

We want to rebuild our beautiful buildings,
Restore our precious lands to their former glory
And raise our flag again.
Not the black and grey it has become from the fires and scorched earth policies,
But a bright blue and gold once again, to fly high and resolute,
In defiance to those who come to try and conquer us.

6. WAR CRIMES. (2022)

One day, may it be soon, Putin and his cohorts will have to pay for the dreadful war crimes they have committed in the name of greed and stupidity.

Four million have crossed the borders,
One man has crossed the lines.
They flee from Russian marauders,
Has he misread the signs?

Show courage in the face of war
You people of Ukraine.
We know you can't take any more,
We pray and feel your pain.

Devastation and desolation
As the land is laid to waste;
Bomb crater holes and some shattered souls,
There's no end but, they are braced!

War crimes committed every day,
By that man at the top.
Shelling hospitals, kids at play,
Can no one make him stop?

Yet another atrocity,
But why, we cannot tell.
Has Putin no shame or pity?
He will go straight to hell!

Devastation and desolation
As more buildings crash and burn.
Bomb crater holes and more shattered souls,
War's evil, will the tide turn?

7. EVIL GENIUS. (2019)

This was written without anyone particular in mind, however it seems to apply rather well to a certain Russian leader; well, at least the first part of the title.

You may be clever, but you've a warped mind,
With depravity of the worst kind.
Your crimes are cunning, undetectable;
A psychopath, and very able.

You are another evil genius,
With a lifestyle that is quite heinous.
Delusions of megalomania,
What on this earth could be zanier?

Somehow you don't seem to need tuition,
As all your plans come to fruition.
You have no regard for body and soul
You always win, as you're in control!

Your blackened heart, your dirty hands, your filthy mind;
There's no escape you're off to hell, and we don't mind.

Those impure thoughts, wicked ideas, your evil ways,
You've been condemned to hell below, for all your days.

For your victims it's scant relief for such acts,
Dead and dying, or left to grieve; these are the facts!

'I wonder how you sleep at night?'
"I don't, and I'm awake and quite
At liberty to plan and scheme;
Then in the day I sleep, and dream!"

8. LIFE OF MISERY. (2022)

I cannot imagine how bad everyday life must be for the poor people in Ukraine, their homes are shattered, there is no electricity or fresh water, food will be in short supply and the winter cold is unforgiving. Spare a thought and be grateful you are not there in the flesh but, please be with them in spirit.

Welcome, to a life of misery
Happily heading to World War Three.
Now, who will be the heir apparent
Once they use the nuclear deterrent?

Ships on the oceans, planes in the sky,
Soldiers on the ground, no one asks why.
People may run but where will they go?
We're fighting an invisible foe.

Will nobody help us in our plight?
We need more weapons, we've got the fight.
We need all the support you can spare –
Is the West afraid of the Russian bear?

Now we live in cellars, underground,
When sirens wail and shells start to pound.
The pictures on the news make me wild,
This is no life for a mother and child.

This war is total insanity,
There is no love or humanity.
Can we flee through a safe corridor
To a safer place? Then we're bombed once more!

9. PEACE IN THE WORLD. (2000)

You can see that this was written over twenty years ago yet the sentiments remain true. Show peace, grace, mercy and respect to all whom you encounter and you won't go too far wrong.

How can there be peace in the world
When there is no peace in your heart?
The troubles you have in yourself
Have repercussions, in every part.

Chorus: Peace in the world
           Make a new start,
           Flags unfurled,
           Love in your heart.
           Take one more step
           Just make amends,
           On your doorstep
           You should have friends.

How can there be peace in the world
When you condone violence in your lane?
Don't say that it doesn't matter –
We need more hope to help our God to reign.

Chorus: …

How can there be peace in the world
When there is conflict with your kin?
Patch up your differences now –
With the true grace that comes from within.

Chorus: …

10. REMEMBRANCE OF WAR SHOULD GENERATE PEACE.
  (2005)

This poem was written for a Remembrance Day some time ago, the title was a thought of mine that the memory of how awful war is ought to make everyone think of peace. Sadly, I was wrong in that estimation.

Is peace just a mirage,
An impossible dream?
How can we quell the rage
That out of hearts can stream?

There's always been conflict,
But do we need such strife?
If we could be more strict
In the running of life...

So, always pray for peace,
Yet turn the other cheek;
To aid the anger cease,
The world's not for the meek!

Though in our faith we're strong,
And we can overcome.
Then correct every wrong
To let your kingdom come.

11. TO THE UNKNOWN TERRORIST. (2009)

We have all heard of the 'Unknown Soldier'. I wrote this while trying to imagine what it must be like to be such a person as a terrorist. How can you relate to somebody who thinks so little of his/her own life that they are prepared to blow themselves to atoms and take along any bystanders who happen to be unfortunate enough to be in their vicinity?
Perhaps it is hard to love those who are so different and don't love us, let alone themselves.

I want to love you
But I don't understand you,
Or your scheming mind.
You sit in your cell
Just waiting to detonate,
A death warrant signed.

Chorus: You are the unknown terrorist,
You want to kill, am I on your list?
Yet you still come, out of the mist…
Isn't it time we made up and kissed?

There must be some good
Though I'm still looking for it.
Or are you possessed
By an evil force,
That can turn your compassion
To passion, at best?

Chorus: ….

Stop what you're doing,
And re-think the agenda
As it makes no sense.
I want to love you
But, oh why, can't you love me
Despite our difference?

12. STONES AND SNARES. (1979)

This is based on the old adage "sticks and stones can break my bones but words can never hurt me" though that may not be entirely true. How many dreams have been shattered by an unkind word from a parent, teacher, even a well meaning friend? Be careful what you say!

Snares and stones may hurt my bones
But let's not hear any moans,
Just keep saying – "It's in the mind"
Or you'll get left far behind.

Sticks and strife, beset your life,
Are you glad you met your wife?
Just keep saying – "I love you lots"
Then you can join all the dots.

Clouds and cares, all through the years
But let's not have any tears,
Just keep saying – "Please dry your eyes"
Life is full of sad goodbyes.

Hurt and harms and lack of charms
May bring you down, load your arms,
Just keep saying – "We rise above"
And give them back perfect love.

13. A CERTAIN WORLD? (2017)

There is nothing certain in this world except death and taxes it is said. Whether you wake up tomorrow is in the lap of the gods, but life is always better with Jesus.

We think we live in a certain world, yet
Although the sun may rise each day,
We do not know upon whom it will set;
Who lives and who's taken away?

But if you hold a certain faith quite strong,
Keep your mind and heart very pure,
The promises that Jesus brings aren't wrong
For you, and won't remain obscure.

For if you read those certain scripture words,
Written down with hope from above;
Then all your tomorrows are so assured,
And will be brought to you with love.

The certainty of death always brings fear,
But in God's image we were made.
So, if your belief is certain and clear,
With God you need not be afraid.

14. DARK FORCES. (2018)

There is more going on in the universe than the best scientists
can adequately explain, dark matter, dark energy even gravity.
Someone once said "There is no such thing as gravity, the earth
sucks!" The quantum world is indeed a mysterious place.

It's gravity that holds us together
And dogma that blows us apart.
Once, I was as light as a feather
Now I'm heavier than a cart!

Things feel solid through electronic forces,
Although it's mostly empty space.
Protons, neutrons, electrons run their courses
Subatomic particles race.

Out in the cosmos where black holes attract,
Event horizon – there things get flatter;
All the supernovae and stars, in fact
Weigh less, the discrepancy is "dark matter".

Our universe expands and goes faster!
And dark energy, what is that?
Are we all hurtling towards disaster,
Our demise, like Schrödinger's cat?

There is so much that we don't understand
It can leave us a bit frightened.
We think of creation, God's mighty hand,
We just need to be more enlightened.

15. LIFE'S LITTLE LUXURIES. (2020)

While thinking of luxuries I realise they are in short supply to our friends in Ukraine. I would, I am afraid, have to take my own roll of toilet tissue.

There's some of life's little luxuries
That I couldn't live without,
Central heating and double glazing
And a teapot with a spout!

Although luxuries are hard to find
Unless you have the cash,
To purchase a palatial mansion
With a pool to make a splash!

I live in the lap of luxury
Here I can ponder my whims,
With a beautiful girl on each arm,
Can you pour another Pimm's?

But all these aren't just luxuries,
A smart suit from my draper,
A flash sporty car to drive real fast,
But best – soft toilet paper!

16. WARMONGERS. (2010)

Throughout history there have been countless wars and rarely does anyone benefit except for those who design bigger and better weapons for killing. Surely if you take a brief glance at history you should realise how pointless and damaging war can be. This is a plea to those who are thinking of going to war or have already started the process; please think again!

Do they know the heartache and misery they bring,
Are they not aware of the fear they cause?
With plotting and fighting and continuing wars,
While onto outdated ideas they cling.

Are they gripped by madness, as their hate does increase,
Is there nothing left, their reason to guide?
Before one more dies, may hardened hearts, stupid pride
Give way to softness, and a lasting peace.

Warmongers are not needed, in a world of peace,
Bring love, not war to all, and bear their load.
Treat the world well and care, it is the only road,
This world's not ours, but our children's on lease.

17. ENOUGH. (2002)

When you reach an age where you should be sensible but still feel you can get away with being daft that means nothing. I still like to have fun and be occasionally irreverent despite my age.

Old enough to know better
Young enough to think why?
Young enough to get wetter
Old enough to stay dry.

Smart enough to do bad stuff
Dumb enough to get caught!
Dumb enough to call your bluff,
Smart enough to leave the port.

Big enough to get spotted
Small enough to get lost.
Small enough to be potted,
Big enough to compost.

Glad enough to keep smiling
Sad enough to make tears.
Sad enough to stop diall'ng,
Glad enough to yell "cheers!"

18. TRAVELLING TOWARDS THE TRUTH. (2014)

We hope that we are all travelling towards truth, and as Pontius Pilate asked Jesus "What is truth?" A fair question, although he did not wait for the answer.

Give me wings of steel that I might fly,
Show me what is real before I die.
I've been all round the world
Talking to boys and girls,
Conversed with learned men
But still don't know the why or when.

Lend me a sturdy ship that I might sail,
Going on a trip it must not fail.
I'm looking for the truth,
Spoken with old and youth,
Sailed to places cold and hot
But I still don't know the why or what.

Help me catch that train that takes me far,
Now I've wracked my brain why we all are.
Keep going down the track
Past my stop and back,
Travelling without a care
Trying to find the why and where.

I've walked up each street, long lane and road
And all that I meet can't break the code.
I've looked in every place
And studied every face,
As there's nothing else to do,
Still can't fathom the why or who.

I've driven in cars, so far and wide
Trawled the all night bars, swallowed my pride.
So many things beside
As I search for a guide,
It has to be there right now;
I'm not given the why and how!

19. OUT OF SIGHT OF LAND. (2017)
(A story about the Viking explorers)

It has always puzzled me why anyone would take a boat and sail into the unknown, thank goodness there are braver and more curious men than me.

Sailing towards the setting sun
In wooden boats and flimsy sails,
An adventure that's just begun,
With Viking oarsmen, hard as nails.
They didn't know if the Earth was round
If the ship foundered, they would be drowned.
Yet they left safe shores to fight and trade
Onward boldly, they were not afraid.

A fair wind and rhythmic rowing
They'd soon be out of sight of land.
How could they know where they're going?
It's one thing I don't understand
They couldn't know where they were heading,
Would they fall off by going too far?
Their culture and influence spreading
Through Europe, Britain, America!

Which bold mariner took that leap,
Heading off into the unknown?
Setting a course over the deep
With no map nor chart and wind blown.
Their ships were built with craft, for such speed,
Coloured shields, axes and battle cries;
They made incursions – the Viking creed,
Looking out for the ultimate prize.

How many perished, no return
To tell their tales of derring-do?
But man must strive and man must learn,
For that is in his nature too.

20. FIRST AND LAST (ONE TO TEN). (2013)

This is just a poem that goes from one to ten in cardinal numbers and ends up with a firing squad!

I remember the first man on the moon,

He once bought a second hand car in June.

When I recalled the Third Reich, I fainted!

And the Forth Bridge is always being painted.

So, I joined a fifth column in China

Developing my sixth sense much finer,

And I was in seventh heaven, until

The Eighth Cavalry rode in for the kill!

I was the ninth to be lined by the wall,

The tenth bullet was the last one of all!

21. A RIDDLE TO ME. (2003)

My wife is a woman, I know that should be fairly obvious but we live in strange times. However, she does sometimes confuse me by changing the subject without due warning (without being sexist it is a girl thing – apparently they are psychic and assume we males are too). Suddenly she is on to another topic and we are conversing at cross purposes, this is what the poem is about.

Talking in a riddle
You expect me to understand,
I'm stuck in the middle –
Of a course uncharted, unplanned.

Chorus: I'm lost out at sea,
Can't see through the fog,
I want to be free!
I'm just a loose cog
With nowhere to go
And nothing to show!

Your language is in code –
And I'm expected to break it,
But I'm up the wrong road,
How am I supposed to make it?

Chorus: …

It's all a mystery
With no clues you want me to solve.
Now it's just history,
You've managed to break my resolve.

Chorus: …

22. THE SCENE OF THE CRIME. (2002)

There are lots of television programmes these days involving
crimes and clever detectives solving them, this is more of a love
story that doesn't quite work out. I do not intend to return to the
scene of the crime!

You set my heart aflame,
How can life be the same
Knowing I love you for all time?
You say I have no claim
On your heart, it's a game –
Having fled the scene of the crime!

You forget I exist,
Yet in my dreams we kissed
And I am feeling in my prime.
I wake and you're not there,
Sometimes life is not fair,
For you've left the scene of the crime.

My mind can't be righted,
A love unrequited …
But I'm wallowing in the slime.
It seems you've long since gone
And my life carries on
I'm still at the scene of the crime.

23. LOST AND FOUND. (2019)

As we age it is becoming more and more of a problem that we lose things. We are constantly inquiring of each other – Where is my phone? What did I come upstairs for? Have you seen the remote? Where the hell's my credit card? I don't think we are losing it just yet but it is very tedious.

There's a hole where the whole should be,
When something precious is lost.
There's a gap; glaring emptiness,
We slump back and count the cost.

Lost love, when it's unrequited,
Lost cause, when you're not invited.
Lost cash, when you can't afford it,
Liberty – you cannot hoard it.

When someone dies the loss is hard.
Losing your mind? Be on your guard!
Losing things is so frustrating,
Relocating; worth the waiting!

Get freedom, your shackles broken,
Find a cause, needs to be spoken.
Finding coins, can leave you reeling,
Finding love, the nicest feeling!

24. ANOTHER DIMENSION? (2020)

*I once knew a guy who did a thesis on tying 10 dimensional knots
in 12 dimensional space! Apparently there are 13 dimensions
although 9 are hidden microscopically within the atomic
structure.*

You move in straight lines, forwards or back,
A linear progression – a track
A graph on a page, no fun in that!
Endlessly, across a world so flat.

However, I am unorthodox,
I started to think outside the box!
Shifting in twists and elegant curves,
Arcs and arches and interesting swerves.

You realise I had to mention,
I've discovered a new dimension!
I can glide in a circular way,
Rolling, swooping like a bird at play.

Although I can scribe circles and rings,
Rounded letters and a host of things.
I'm still trapped in a singular plane,
The third dimension beyond my brain.

Perhaps your world isn't like a sheet,
A solid shape I would love to meet.
A cube, a globe even a brick,
Pyramid or dome – that would be slick.

For then much to my consternation,
Far beyond my imagination.
Stay in place, with no wish to blunder,
How many dimensions, I wonder?

Apparently there are eleven,
But the four we have makes up heaven.
Try tying a ten dimensional knot
In the twelve dimensional space we've got?

25. SOMETHING BETTER. (2021)

To date I have written over 820 poems and I am always striving to pen a better one that will make me as famous as Wordsworth. Well, I can dream can't I?

It must be a sign of something better
If I can sit down and write a letter.
There are 26 to choose from; absurd?
Tomorrow I may complete a whole word!

Chorus: It's amazing, as I take stock,
          A slight race against the clock;
          Keep writing, the mind to unlock
          It's the cure for writers' block!

Then if one small word leads to a second,
I'll make a sentence, before you reckoned,
I may have to stifle a laugh –
As I reach the end of a paragraph.

Chorus: …

For days I have remained lost in my thoughts,
Played music, seen films and even watched sports.
My muse ran off, there's no way to get her,
Tomorrow I hope for something better!

Chorus: …

26. CHOP AND CHANGE. (2021)
(A tale of Henry VIII and his wives)

Henry was a king with a single mind; if he disagreed with the status quo he would change it to suit his purposes. So, when he couldn't divorce his first wife, because the pope would not sanction such a thing, he broke away from the church of Rome and started his own. He also removed the heads of two of his wives because they failed to provide a male heir; shame he didn't know it is the male who determines the sex of children.

Do I chop and change to gain a wife?
Once I loved her but she brings me strife,
With no son and heir, she'll have to go.
I'll write to the pope to make it so.

Chorus: Some I change, others I chop,
I'm the king no one can stop.
My foul plan to get a bride,
Yet Rome is not on my side!

So I'll change and chop religion's course,
Get new archbishops to grant divorce.
This is one battle I must win,
Then I can move on, with Anne Boleyn.

Chorus: …

Soon I tire of her, boring in bed,
Try her for treason, off with her head!
I must begin all over again,
Though I've found a maid who is called Jane.

Chorus: …

Harrah! She gave birth to a fine son
Then died soon after, the court to stun.
I'm looking abroad to Anne of Cleves,
But she's so ugly, I hope she leaves!

Chorus: …

Another divorce is on the cards,
Call the clergy and summon the guards!
A second Catherine would fit the bill
A young girl I can bend to my will.

Chorus: …

She has a lover it's reputed,
So, she'll have to be executed.
A third Katherine and she's not the worst
Though she survived me, for I died first!

Chorus: …

Six wives, a shame it wasn't seven,
One each day of the week in heaven!
Though my wanton lust and wicked ways
Means that down in hell, I spend my days!

27. 50% OF NOTHING. (2020)

*Half of nothing is still nothing; this poem introduces the word
half a number of times and ignores the concept of zero
completely.*

It was a half-baked idea
That went off half-cocked,
Some were a bit half-hearted here,
The others just mocked.

Then my other half tried to moan,
She had much to do.
I'd half a mind to go alone
Then to meet the few.

When the strangest thoughts make no sense
Who said "Half a mo!"?
It's no good sitting on the fence
With half way to go.

There are no half measures in our
Half-timbered dwelling,
Bought at half price, but turning sour?
That would be telling.

Here half truths sell for half a crown,
There is no half way.
The flag at half-mast or cut down,
This is not our day.

Live a half-life of half measure,
Or die in glory!
Don't be half-dead – look for treasure,
Or there's no story.

28. I.D. (2021)

We live in a world obsessed with numbers and identification, do you know who you are? There is a story of a famous and pompous individual at an airport trying to get a ticket for an earlier flight with little success. Finally in a fit of exasperation he blurts out "Do you know who I am?"
With great aplomb the girl at the desk responded "Can anyone here help, this gentleman appears to have forgotten who he is!"

"Have you got ID?
Can you tell me who you are?
Just run it by me,
Now I've stopped your car!"

"Show me your papers please,
Your licence and passport too.
Insurance I'll seize,
While you wonder what to do."

"It seems in order,
So, where are you heading for?"
Stopped at the border,
This is becoming a chore.

'Am I free to go?'
But that mean look in his eyes…
"Now I think you know
I will have to breathalyse!"

My heart starts to sink,
Because they know who I am.
I have had a drink,
Now I am really in a jam!

29. DIGGING DOWN, DELVING DEEP. (2021)

It would seem I have watched too many programmes about archaeology.

It was an ancient baby,
From ancient Babylon;
The bones and skull left for me
Although the flesh was gone.

Chorus: For I'm an archaeologist,
       I dig things up for a living.
       There are so many sites on my list –
       And the earth is always giving!

How he lived is just a haze
I don't know how he died,
I'm sure in those far off days
His mother must have cried.

Among the scattered bones, rocks
And shards of pottery,
Nothing lies that really shocks
It's history's lottery.

When you're born, the life you lead
Down to the hands of fate,
What went on in your head
We can only speculate.

We know little of your time,
Until you've been unearthed.
You should have been in your prime,
But now your second birth!

Digging deep, more artefacts
And relics by the score;
We can piece together facts,
That way we learn much more.

Chorus: ….

30. THE SHIPWRECK. (2021)

*This poem came about as I was attempting to produce a dramatic
visual piece, a storm at sea might have been a good place to
begin.*

The storm is raging, the waves crash down,
The rain is lashing from a black sky.
Grab tightly the mast or you will drown,
Hang on to the helm, the spume does fly.

Now haul down the sails, and hold our course;
Two on the tiller, straining with might,
But the wind blows hard, increasing force,
Surge mountainous waves, their crests flecked white!

Loud crack! The mast snapped, tangle of ropes
Writhe across the deck, into the sea,
A whirling maelstrom of fading hopes
As the wind whips up, our spirits flee.

Orders are screamed, lost in the gale,
Waves rise with menace the wind just mocks;
The timbers shudder, faces turn pale,
Out of darkness, heading for rocks!

With splintering sound we smash into shore,
We're wrecked on a reef, jagged outcrop.
Beams break like matchsticks, in a beast's maw.
A ship now shattered, waves overtop!

The flotsam is strewn on the shoreline,
Another vessel claimed by Neptune.
Men, cargo and ship lost in brine,
Sailing adventure ending too soon!

31. REMOTE ISLANDS. (2021)

My wife and I had a lovely holiday on the east coast of Scotland a couple of years back, we stayed in a fisherman's cottage over-looking a variety of islands that monks once stayed on. I was trying to imagine the isolation, hardship and loneliness on such a remote island, completely cut off from civilisation.

Virtually inaccessible,
Small, but perfectly made.
Sheer cliffs loom from a choppy sea
So, should I be afraid?

Completely uninhabited,
Just sea birds and the seals.
Lonely, away from company,
They say 'solitude heals!'

A craggy rock above the waves,
A missed step, I'd be sunk.
You may wonder what I'm here for
But I'm a hermit monk!

The more remote the island is
All the better for me,
Because you are never all alone,
I think you must agree?

32. BULLY ME NOT, BULLY FOR YOU! (2021)

Bullying is not nice at school or in the workplace or indeed in the wider world, sadly it goes on. This was written as attempt to prevent school bullies getting the upper hand.

Sticks and stones should never be used,
Even your thoughts can leave me bruised!
Nobody likes to be abused,
So be kind and let's all smile.

Chorus: Not in the playground nor in the park,
        Not in daytime never after dark.
        Not in a large gang or on your own
        Don't say words when you use the wrong tone.
        Not on a mobile or a device,
        Bully me not – it's not very nice!
        Though I'm different, I'm part of the crowd,
        I won't be bullied, I won't be bowed.

Some words are better not spoken,
Are rules just made to be broken?
Love should be there as a token
To make all our lives worthwhile.

Chorus: …

If you bully, lives will be wrecked
No need to remain so hen-pecked;
Show more compassion and respect
And then go the extra mile!

Chorus: …

33. ON HER OWN. (2021)

This was written as a general observation of loneliness which is as much a danger to health as smoking 15 cigarettes daily. I belong to a nationwide charity called "Linking Lives" which endeavours to match lonely people with a regular friend who can visit. You just need to stay an hour or so once a week and keep in touch and it is well worth the minimal effort.

There is a family, but they live far away,
She had a husband, though long since passed away.
She's on her own now, one of the lonely maids,
Lost in her own thoughts, as her memory fades…

Living in the past, youthful recollections
Often come to mind, some early selections.
The future missing, no point to tomorrow
All her friends are gone, she's living in sorrow.

No carers visit, is there no one that cares;
Just a friendly face, to check on how she fares?
Once she was someone, mother, worker and wife,
Now frail and fading, with no one in her life.

Each sad day she waits, for death to come calling,
He's on his way now, no needing for stalling.
Another lost soul to add to his vast count!
She'll go without trace as his numbers just mount.

So, what about you, could you not be a friend?
Have you compassion, a kindly heart to lend –
To provide the joy company brings and more,
And if you can help, what are you waiting for!

34. SEEING STARS. (2021)

I did once walk into a lamppost when I wasn't keeping my eyes on where I was going, it hurt and I saw stars. However, the rest of the tale is made up as I quickly carried on hoping no one observed my stupidity.

I wasn't looking up
It wasn't even nighttime,
But I saw stars!
I don't study the heavens
I am not an astronomer,
But I still saw stars!

I'm not superstitious
Never read my horoscope,
But I saw stars!
I like art, Vincent van Gogh
I have a print of "Sunflowers"
But a starry night?

I was reading a book…
And I walked into a lamppost.
Then I saw stars!!
I recoiled and then collapsed
Falling down into a black hole –
And there were no stars?

A sharp blow to the head
Can jar and cause confusion,
Makes you see stars.
Though mine were a mystery,
I wonder which constellation
Contain all my stars?

Now I have a headache,
People are helping me up –
They are real stars.
I should look where I'm going
Cease walking into hard objects,
I don't like those stars!!

35. NO FUN, ARTHRITIS! (2021)

Arthritis is very common and it gets worse as you age, it's no fun.

I squat right down
And my knees give a creak,
I bend slightly
Then my back gives a tweak,
This will happen
Every day of the week!
It's no fun getting old.

I try to reach
All the way to my toe,
I don't get far
The movement doesn't flow,
And arthritis
Is such a painful foe.
It's no fun getting stiff.

Chorus: With arthritis my body is riddled
   And everything else is failing,
   I feel so certain that I've been diddled
   For my coffin lid needs nailing!

I stretch on round
And there's a painful click,
I'd love to run
But that's not a good trick,
A slow hobble
Now that gets on my wick!
It's no fun slowing down.

My neck won't turn
In either direction,
I still have nerves
But they've lost connection;
My joints crumble
I've lost my perfection.
No fun this arthritis!

Chorus: …

36. AMORPHOUS BLOB. (2021)

*King or queen, peasant or pauper, we all start life as a bundle of
cells, a shapeless mass or, as I put it, an amorphous blob.*

You begin as an amorphous blob,
Two minute cells of indistinct form.
Then dividing, they do a good job
And differentiate like a storm.
It's strange to watch the patterns emerge
As things become tissues and glands.
The process more complex as cells merge
To produce life? No one understands.

Chorus: Whether you're a top knob, or a down and out slob,
        We all begin life as an amorphous blob!
        Airs and graces just fall, fat or thin, short or tall
        It's a miracle that you are born at all.

Yet millions of seeds scatter, then swim
Across an ocean, starting a trend,
Only one makes it, the rest go dim,
And the union is made in the end.
Thus another life is made complete,
You have your life, now would you trade it?
But you should be proud of such a feat,
As you're the only one that made it!

Chorus: …

It's survival of the fast and first
And against you all the odds are stacked.
Don't imagine you are forever cursed
For you're the one the angels backed.
It really is a jungle out there,
But as usual, nature knows best.
A life like yours is a thing so rare,
Being here you passed the hardest test!

Chorus: …

37. BOUNCE BACK. (2021)

This is a poem about how we are misusing our planet; maybe the earth will bounce back from what we are doing to it. Though I imagine it will do it when we are driven to extinction.

We trip the light fantastic
Though everything is plastic,
The world is not elastic
It won't recover from the things we do.

The waste we're throwing away,
Resources used up each day;
Won't be long before we pay
For the short-sighted greed from me and you!

Chorus: We're hoping the seas will bounce back
        But we may have gone too far.
        The rivers are clogged and moaning,
        Climate change starting to jar!
        We trusted the Earth would forgive,
        With a heart as hard as flint,
        But we're really in a mess
        Please curb your carbon footprint!

Gone, our good reputations
Across this and all nations.
Now waiting at the stations
Throwing good money after HS2!

We need lots more renewal,
Not burning fossil fuel;
For green's a colour so cool,
And the end of the line looks black, not blue!

Chorus: …

38. ENOUGH TO GO ROUND. (2021)

I have always been of the opinion that there has been sufficient
money, food and resources to go around, sadly they are mostly in
the wrong place or the wrong hands. Perhaps the current crisis
we are experiencing is a hint of making a change to live a better
way and share.

It's like a sport, when fuel is short,
Jump in your car to panic buy!
On the forecourt, so much you bought,
Don't you ever think, or wonder why?

Lack in the shop, pile to the top
Your trolley, with things you don't need –
You just can't stop, until you drop
With so many hungry mouths to feed!

Chorus: There's always enough to go round,
It's just in the wrong places!
But give, share and be kind I've found
Brings smiles to relieved faces.

The well runs dry, no rain is nigh
Your livestock and crops are dying.
A cloudless sky, the soil so dry
And it's not for the want of trying…

Money soon goes, add to our woes
Cost of living always rising.
I need more clothes, but just suppose
We shared, would that be so surprising?

Chorus: …

39. POSITIVE FORCE. (2021)

Sometimes it is difficult to keep a smile on your face when the whole world appears to be turning to excrement. But be strong and have a good heart and try to encourage those who are struggling to make their lives better in any way that you can. We are here to serve our fellow man and live the life that Jesus showed us to be the way.

Be a positive force, in a negative world;
With God in your corner you will not go wrong.
Send out all the goodness and exhibit more love,
With happiness and joy we can all get along.

Be a beacon of hope, in a despairing world,
With Jesus on your side, you won't face defeat.
Continue with strong faith, dispel gathering gloom,
And bring a real smile to everyone you greet.

Be a vessel of truth, in this twisted world,
With the Spirit in you, you know that it's right.
Correct wrongs where you can, and speak truth from the word,
Then you can lift poor souls away from endless blight.

You can't do it alone you'll need strength from above;
Start each day with a prayer, and notions of love.
Bring good to the hateful, and help those in distress,
Then when you course is run, we'll know you're a success.

40. COLLECTIVE NOUNS. (2021)

There are many collective nouns, some are alliterative, others just plain weird. I am not sure whether a committee sat for hours choosing the oddest combinations, but I had a bit of fun composing the story.

A gaggle of geese, waddle along the road,
Perhaps we should have a giggle of comedians? Alliterative and amusing.
Not to mention a goggle of TV viewers, glued to their screens.
Or a guggle of gargoyles, glaring from guttering.
I don't think geggle is a word!

A pride of lions – should it not be a roar or a lust?
A sloth of slugs, silently, slither so slowly
Towards a devastation of deadly sins.
Is an unkindness of ravens better, than a murder of crows?
Leave the decisions to the parliament of owls!

Believe it or not it is an armoury of aardvark;
Then a troop of soldiers with a quiver of arrows,
And a battery of guns, dodge a hail of bullets.
Spewing up a cloud of dust in a range of mountains,
Possibly waiting to meet a host of angels!

A crew of sailors, in a fleet of ships,
With a company of actors and a galaxy of stars.
Some play with a pack of cards and cackle like hyenas.
One reads an anthology of poems about a plague of locusts,
And the mischief of mice and men!

A swarm of bees buzz and a lounge of lizards relax,
I recall a memory of elephants and hear a crash of rhinoceroses,
While watching a crossing of zebras, with the wisdom of wombats.
Instantly, an intrusion of cockroaches attracts a sloth of bears –
Wait, what happened to those slugs?

41. MOMENTOUS. (2021)

My eldest son and his wife have recently provided us with our first granddaughter, on his birthday – "Best present ever!" he was to exclaim.
This is a conundrum about how do we think before we have words? How does our memory work? Then why does it start failing as we age? Looking at babies I am certain that they are born with all the knowledge of the universe and gradually lose it by the time they start to talk.

That first moment, a breath, a gasp, a cry…
A new experience, my first day.
But I don't recall it, I wonder why?
A momentous event, they say.

Though the memory of it escapes me now;
Did I know when thoughts were unformed?
Those fleeting minutes of pain, that somehow
Through this body arose and stormed,

To disappear as swiftly as a blink;
Leaving no trace in memory banks.
A murky mist I grope into to think;
For the memories of others, give thanks!

But I'm here. That's something you can't deny,
Despite my lack of clear recall.
Observe, my actual birth was not a lie
Though my recollections are small.

Now close to death, my memory is failing,
I await the final curtain.
I drift in the past, lucid regaling;
Although nothing is quite certain.

42. SHARP TONGUES. (2021)

Insults can be quite cutting and a discouraging word can be extremely damaging, although if I was facing a mad axe man I would prefer to be armed with a sword or spear than rely on my wit, wisdom and wordiness.

The sharpest of all weapons is the tongue;
Nags at the elderly, snaps at the young.
Bites the hand that feeds it, harsh words are wrung.
The pen, mightier than the sword, perhaps!
But beware the edge of the tongue that flaps!

The worst of all weapons are spiteful words,
When that tirade bursts forth in flocks or herds…
Pecking and clawing, just like angry birds!
Written words can be like a love token,
Beware those that are hatefully spoken.

The skilful words that come from lying lips,
More hurtful than lashing from leather whips;
Wounding deep but, often passed off as quips!
So be more truthful in all your dealings,
Just curb truth to save someone's feelings.

Hold your tongue, bite your lip, keep words inside;
Don't use speech that can hurt, split or divide.
Honour love, and let conscience be your guide.
If you wish to avoid depravity
Do take care of your oral cavity!

43. ELEPHANTS' GRAVEYARD. (2022)

*There are apocryphal stories of elephants' graveyards in secret
places in Africa, though I don't believe any have been discovered.
Certainly elephants are intelligent creatures and do mourn when
one of the herd dies and have rituals associated with that.
This was written as I was thinking about those majestic animals,
and how sad it is that their number is dwindling, due to poachers
who indiscriminately kill them for the ivory found in their tusks.*

Enormous tusks and giant bones,
Here only skeletons rest and lie.
A secret place among the stones –
This is where elephants come to die!

Pachyderms pack a punch indeed,
They can weigh 6 tons, stand 10 feet tall!
They use their tusks and trunks to feed,
They're poached for ivory – numbers fall.

Elephants don't bury their dead,
Elderly leave for this resting place.
They never forget, it is said;
Despite their size, they don't leave much trace.

The herd always stick together,
They have rituals and they do grieve.
Walk miles whatever the weather.
I wonder what other tales they weave?

44. INFLATION. (2022)

We are now officially in a recession, the pandemic, the war in Ukraine and 'Brexit' have all had their part to play in the economy. Not being an accountant I cannot tell you where to invest your money for the best returns, but I do know that inflation is bad. As I open the poem inflation is good for balloons but not for the pound in your pocket. That's assuming you even have a coin of the realm or indeed a pair of trousers with a pocket to place it in?

Inflation, it's good for balloons,
Important for the waxing of moons.
You'll wonder where your money went
When it's running over six per cent!

Inflation, made the "Big Bang" go,
Bankers want to keep inflation low.
So that our wages can keep pace,
No one desires inflation to race.

And now we feel like we're in a crusher,
There's no more gas being piped in from Russia.
Food rotting in ports and petrol costs rise,
It's a triple whammy – and there's no prize!

Why don't we just print more money,
That's surreal, like the Easter bunny?
Excuse me, but I'll have to dash
Loaves of bread cost a bucket of cash!

Inflation, good for my ego,
Dread follows us, wherever we go.
If I'm short of cash – what the heck!
I can always write another cheque!!

Money and wealth it seems like an obsession
Are we heading for global recession?
I work hard and save, but is that a crime?
Now I'm broke – brother, can you spare a dime?

45. LIFE COULD BE GRAND. (2022)

*This country is in trouble – the NHS is collapsing, the unions are
striking, the immigrants are invading and we have a government
that does nothing sensible.*
*The latest crackpot idea is to send illegal boat people over to
Rwanda, this has not been easy to implement nor has it put off
those who come over in unseaworthy rafts! The energies should
be used to tackle the evil ones who take money for people
trafficking and provide sub-standard crafts to cross a short but
very dangerous stretch of sea.*

They'd like to see them endangered, like the panda,
Not coming to our shores on an inflatable lander.
Who had the brainwave – "Let's send them to Rwanda?"
Now we're in splendid isolation, and life is grander.

Chorus:
Won't life be grand
When they're stuck in a landlocked land?
This wasn't planned,
Won't someone lend a helping hand?
So ease the pain,
They won't be coming back again.
We'll keep our rain,
Next time send them to the Ukraine!

So ask the average person where Rwanda lies,
They might well say "Somewhere in Africa I would surmise."
Do we no longer listen to their anguished cries?
Out of sight is out of mind; why don't they try it for size?

Chorus: …

So, it would be cheaper to send them to the Ritz.
Politicians speak – it's not the way of us Brits,
What to do in Kigali, eat banana splits?
Hardly a free holiday, it's not pretty, it's the pits!

Chorus: …

46. DON'T TALK OF TOMORROW. (2022)

Watching historical programmes often makes me consider what life must have been like in olden times. This is the story of somebody who is on death row for a minor misdemeanour and is contemplating what lies in store in the morning.

Talk about tomorrow?
That will only bring me sorrow,
In a life that's almost hollow;
So, talk of something else!

Talk now of yesterday,
When all my days were not so grey,
But in the past I cannot stay.
Please, talk of something else!

Thinking now of today,
The deed is done, now I must pay.
From an honest life I did stray.
Now think of something else!

Only a week ago
I was quite free from all this woe,
But now the fear begins to grow.
Oh, think of something else!

In the morning I'll die,
I'll go to my doom with a sigh;
My imminent demise is nigh.
Wish I was somewhere else!

47. ARE WE ALL ALONE? (2022)

Someone once remarked – "If there is intelligent life somewhere out in the universe, that is scary; and if we are all alone and unique that is even more scary." There are hundreds of millions of stars some of which have planets, so statistically it is possible life has occurred elsewhere. However, I do not believe that we have been visited by aliens, as the distances between galaxies are just too far. The likelihood is, if they are anything like us, they would have invented the atomic bomb and blown their world and themselves up.

Are we alone in the universe,
Is man the pinnacle of success?
Or do the galaxies teem with life?
For either way, we are in a mess!

Somewhere, maybe sentient beings
Looking out, with the same pondering thoughts;
They could be weird alien creatures,
Or is Earth one of the last resorts?

Life could be almost ubiquitous,
But likely to be a simple kind.
Plants and single cells – extremophiles
On a hostile world we may soon find!

Now the chances of intelligence
Appears to be vanishingly small,
They won't have had time to develop
They've hit an evolutionary wall!

Even if there may be clever ones,
They're too far away to waste their wits
Conquering space or travelling to us.
Doubtless they've blown each other to bits!!

48. CRYPTIC WAVE. (2022)

*Light is more complex than we first thought, it may be a particle
or a wave, and in the quantum world it is both. Apparently it
does carry information and God created it so he could see what
he was doing!*

Can it be a particle,
Or is it a cryptic wave?
Anyone who defines that
Is confused or rather brave.

For as light goes through a slit
It can decide what to be;
If you try to predict it
It may change, for it is free!

It's a quantum world we live in
Where nothing is what it seems.
It's a strange, 'quarky' and quirky
Place to scramble all your dreams.

Quantum entanglement shows
Spooky effects at distance,
How really nobody knows…
Not at Einstein's insistence.

Then in a quantum vacuum,
Photons appear in the void,
But there's nothing in the room;
As they're instantly destroyed!

It's a quantum world we live in,
Where reality is dead.
To try to unscramble the facts
We're just left shaking our head!

49. RANTER AND RAVER. (2022)

These two do not exist but for arguments sake here they are!

There was a man called Ranter
Who was skilled in banter
And argued every day.
He would rant with bad intent
Starting an argument,
He always got his way!

>There's another called Raver,
>He would never quaver,
>But yelled and shook his fist.
>He bellowed on for ages
>With both fools and sages
>So very few he missed!

That person known as Ranter,
Even upset Santa
And got no gifts that year.
He shouted at the elves
Told them to f*** themselves!
He really doesn't care!

>That man who was named Raver
>Please do us a favour–
>Silence your tongue that twists.
>You should try to keep quiet
>Not incite a riot;
>You're on the naughty lists!

There was a man called Ranter
Spewed out hate at a canter,
We gave him dirty looks!
With such soapbox invective,
Should be more selective,
You're not in our good books!

>Here's to that man called Raver
>Speeches not to savour,
>Raved like a lunatic!
>He tried to cross the border,
>A restraining order
>Confines him to the 'nick'.

50. LOVERS DISSOLVED IN TEARS. Part 2 (1974/2022)

As you can see I wrote the first and last verses of this poem in 1974, that's almost 50 years ago! It is one of my favourite and I have always wanted to extend it to another verse or two, and now I have.

Well they loved so much,
And they loved for years;
That when they died
The whole world cried,
And dissolved those lovers in tears.

Why that lovers' touch
Took away all fears,
On their demise
The whole world cries
A lachrymal solution, dear.

Well they loved so much,
On that fateful day
Bodies mingle,
Now not single
As together, they float away.

Their love was such,
Though their bodies gone,
Love couldn't die
And brought a sigh
To all who loved another one.

51. CANCELLED CHRISTMAS. (2022)

*I am no Christmas Grinch but, this year things were looking
somewhat grim coming into the festive season so hence the poem.
For Christmas lunch, as an austerity measure, I often suggest
beans on toast with a sprig of holly; a tasty, nutritious and less
fattening option!*

There's no turkey this year, bird flu took care of that,
With avian flu no goose is getting fat!
A shortage of fir trees and no baubles to hang,
Christmas this year will not be going with a bang?

Shops aren't selling tinsel, crackers are left on the shelf,
There are no toys being made by any little elf.
You should block your chimney, Santa's not coming down;
There's no drink or parties, everyone's wearing a frown.

I'm not sending cards out the postage is too steep,
I can't afford presents, my debts in too deep!
It should be a happy time, but it makes me weep;
I'll just miss Christmas Day, I'll probably stay asleep!

So cull all the reindeer, ban Nativity plays!
Santa can now retire for the rest of his days.
It is no longer the season to be jolly,
It will be beans on toast with a sprig of holly!

It's going to be darker in a dark time of year,
Electric bills so high, there's no light anywhere.
We'll need to follow the rules of Oliver Cromwell
And cancel Christmas – maybe Easter as well!

52. WARM PLACES. (2022)

With cost of heating so high many folk are debating whether to have the heat on, off or turned down or miss a hot meal. Tragic in this day and age! Here is a man who wished for warmth and ended up somewhere slightly hotter, and I don't mean the Maldives.

So, I'm looking for a warm space
Now I have turned down the heating!
Wrap myself in a blanket's grace,
But the warmth is only fleeting.

It's freezing and started to snow,
The pubs are closed, that is dozy;
The shops gone, there's nowhere to go!
I just need somewhere more cosy.

Wait! Here's a man who looks quite hot,
And he's got me under his spell.
Invites me to a real warm spot,
Blazing fires; hold on… this is Hell!

No longer warm, but all sweaty,
And being tortured with hate an'
My tears falling like confetti;
For this is the realm of Satan!!

I wish I was back in my flat,
I wouldn't complain of the cold;
I would whack up the thermostat,
Then fret about bills when I'm old.

53. STRAINING EVERY SINEW (2018)
(THE STRONGEST MEN)

I enjoy watching "The world's strongest man" on TV, despite being the original 9 stone weakling (60 kilos). Recently it was won by the mighty Tom Stoltman from Scotland (6 foot 8 or 2.04m and weighing in at 156 kilos). However, in equal second place was the Ukrainian Oleksii Novikov who having been on the front line fighting against the Russian invaders was limited in his training – what an incredible effort!

Straining every sinew
Giving all that's in you,
And can you continue
When pains get severe?

Pulling, pushing, lifting,
Keep your mind from drifting,
Kegs and sacks need shifting
Mistakes cost you dear!

Heavy trucks need hauling,
Like through treacle crawling;
The aches are appalling,
Still metres to go.

Atlas stones need clearing,
Then the pain gets searing,
Only loss they're fearing,
Losing is such woe.

Men with bulging muscles
Enjoy battle tussles
And every beard rustles,
Eating huge dinners.

Then panting and puffing
They almost lose stuffing!
Realise only toughing
It out, means winners!

54. LOVE CAN OVERCOME. (2022)

The last offering in this volume is an uplifting one and is dedicated to the people still in Ukraine as well as those who have fled. They may be living very different lives in strange circumstances and I hope they are being well cared for. Soon, I hope, as we all do, the war will end and they may return to rebuild their country and their lives.

When all your troubles make you numb,
We may say that "All things will pass."
However, more problems amass,
Then only love can overcome.

Poverty keeps you in the slum,
Though riches are not what you need.
Share and survive; for that's our creed!
For only love can overcome.

When words of hate strike you dumb,
All your battles may seem lost.
Pray, do not grieve nor count the cost,
As only love can overcome.

Finally death? Don't look so glum,
Because you are merely mortal.
You must face that fearful portal,
Yet only love will overcome!

BIOGRAPHY

Richard was born in Chiswick, London the product of a Cumbrian mother, from Egremont, and a Polish father. His father hailed from the small town of Jarosław in south eastern Poland a mere 30 miles from the Ukrainian border; which provides a real connection with the people of Ukraine. His father was studying law at Vilnius university when the Second World War broke out, he was taken with many of the intellectuals to a Siberian labour camp, under the orders of Stalin. He never liked the Russians after that, and after the war, having fought with the Allies in North Africa and at Monte Cassino in Italy, he decided to come to England rather than return to Poland, at that time under Russian occupation.

Following qualification from the Anglo-European College of Chiropractic, in Bournemouth, Richard worked as a chiropractor in Harrow for forty years, and has a Master's degree in paediatrics as well as studying kinesiology and cranial techniques. During his working life he saw patients from over thirty different countries, as well as lecturing at the chiropractic college, writing a number of original research papers and visiting Europe and the USA as a speaker at international conferences.

Now retired with wife Cathy in Cockermouth, they have three grown-up sons; one of whom resides locally and has a daughter, one who lives in Gibraltar with a son and step-son, and the youngest who has emigrated to Australia and is engaged to an Australian girl.

Richard's interests include science, travel, DIY and sport, particularly football, cricket and martial arts, he enjoys quizzing and he loves dogs. He is a lay preacher at his local church, a governor at the nearby primary school, a volunteer at the local food bank and writes poetry on a diverse range of topics as a way to relax. He is a lifelong scholar, a family orientated man, an innovative and creative personality with an irrepressible and irreverent sense of humour.